INSTANT HAPPY Notes

AND OTHER SURPRISES TO MAKE YOU SMILE

sourcebooks

P9-BJE-774

Copyright © 2017 by Sourcebooks, Inc.
Cover and internal design © 2017 by Sourcebooks, Inc.
Internal artwork by individual artists: John Aardema, Bridget M. Alexander, Elizabeth Boyer, Susan Busch, Catherine Casalino Design, Jennifer K. Beal Davis, Matt Davis, Maggie Edkins, Cassie Gutman, Travis Hasenour, Nicole Hower, Krista Joy Johnson, Kelly Lawler, Michelle McAvoy, Danielle McNaughton, Lin Miceli, Benjamin Nelson, Kay Birkner, Heather Morris, Bethany Orlowski, Ben Ouart, Jenna Quatraro, Jillian Rahn, Kerri Resnick, Kandi Rich, Tina Silva, Becca Sage, Eliza Smith, Allison Sundstrom, Amanda Skolek, Brittany Vibbert, Christine Webster
Internal images © Freepik.com, Unsplash.com, Merfin/GettyImages, sundrawalex/GettyImages, Vit_Mar/GettyImages, Vanzyst/GettyImages, Ukususha/Thinkstock, Julia_Henze/Thinkstock, Vioricalonescu/Thinkstock, speakingtomato/Thinkstock, artJazz/Thinkstock, topform84/Thinkstock, beatpavel/Thinkstock, Martyshova/Thinkstock, yayayoyo/Thinkstock, Lostanastacia/Thinkstock, nata789/Thinkstock, chereshneva/Thinkstock

Published by Sourcebooks, Inc.
P.O. Box 4410, Naperville, Illinois 60567-4410
(630) 961-3900
Fax: (630) 961-2168
www.sourcebooks.com

Printed and bound in China.
LEO 10 9 8 7 6 5 4 3 2 1

A DAY WITHOUT

LAUGHTER

IS A DAY

WASTED

This collection of notes has been lovingly created by the dreamers, designers, and artists at Sourcebooks for you, our readers. Plus, we were able to include work from a number of friends who share our belief that books change lives. Each unique design is a vision from one of the many people who have the privilege of making books every day. We hope the notes within spark true happiness and create the unique magic only found between the pages of a book.

Thank you

for being a part of our story—now go get happy!

Brittany Vibbert, Art Director

Meaghan Gibbons, Editor

BRIGHTEN UP YOUR DAY

boost the happiness around you with these feel-good notes! You'll find unexpected compliments, much-needed encouragement, lighthearted fun, and silly doodles that are sure to make you grin. The sole purpose of this chunky, compact book is to boost your mood—just think of it as your best friend who will bring you instant happy wherever you go!

THE BEST WAY TO PREDICT THE FUTURE IS TO CREATE IT

—ABRAHAM LINCOLN

Every Day *is a* Fresh START

Light tomorrow with today.

Elizabeth Barrett Browning

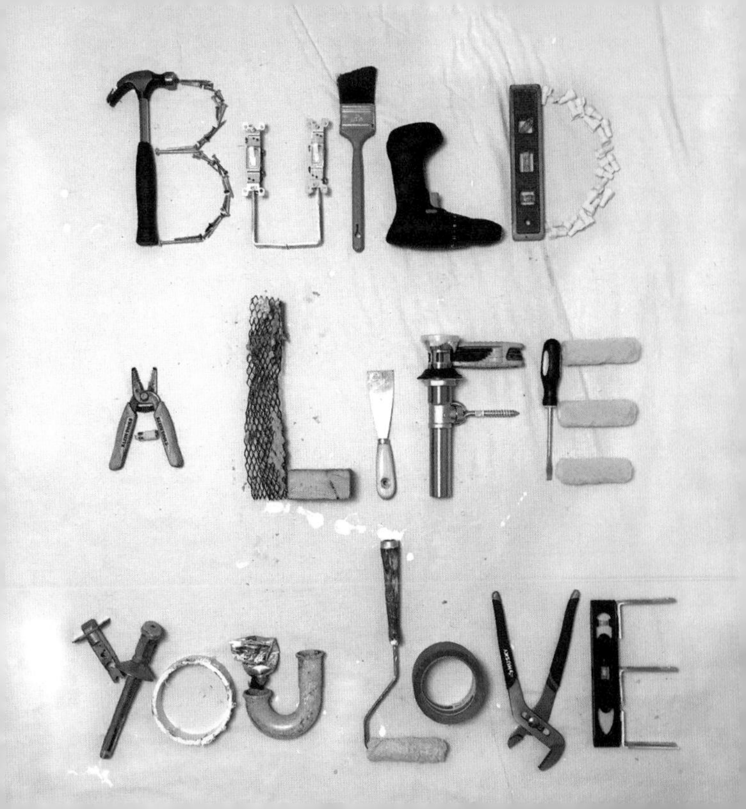
BUILD
A LIFE
YOU LOVE

IT'S OK TO TAKE A BREAK

CARPE THAT DIEM!

TRUST
YOURSELF
COMPLETELY

INSTANT HAPPY
Notes

AND OTHER SURPRISES
TO MAKE YOU SMILE

S sourcebooks

Sourcebooks and the colophon are registered trademarks of Sourcebooks, Inc.

Published by Sourcebooks, Inc.
P.O. Box 4410, Naperville, Illinois 60567-4410
(630) 961-3900
Fax: (630) 961-2168
www.sourcebooks.com

Printed and bound in China.
LEO 10 9 8 7 6 5 4 3 2 1

A DAY WITHOUT LAUGHTER IS A DAY WASTED

This collection of notes has been lovingly created by the dreamers, designers, and artists at Sourcebooks for you, our readers. Plus, we were able to include work from a number of friends who share our belief that books change lives. Each unique design is a vision from one of the many people who have the privilege of making books every day. We hope the notes within spark true happiness and create the unique magic only found between the pages of a book.

Thank you

for being a part of our story—now go get happy!

Brittany Vibbert

Meaghan Gibbons

Brittany Vibbert, Art Director   Meaghan Gibbons, Editor

BRIGHTEN UP YOUR DAY

boost the happiness around you with these feel-good notes! You'll find unexpected compliments, much-needed encouragement, lighthearted fun, and silly doodles that are sure to make you grin. The sole purpose of this chunky, compact book is to boost your mood—just think of it as your best friend who will bring you instant happy wherever you go!

TAKE THE

Scenic

route

THE BEST WAY TO PREDICT THE FUTURE IS TO CREATE IT

—ABRAHAM LINCOLN

let go, move forward.

NOONE ME
EXPECTED ME.
EVERYTHING
ME.
AWAITED ME.
— PSMITH

Every Day IS A Fresh START

Light tomorrow with today.

Elizabeth Barrett Browning

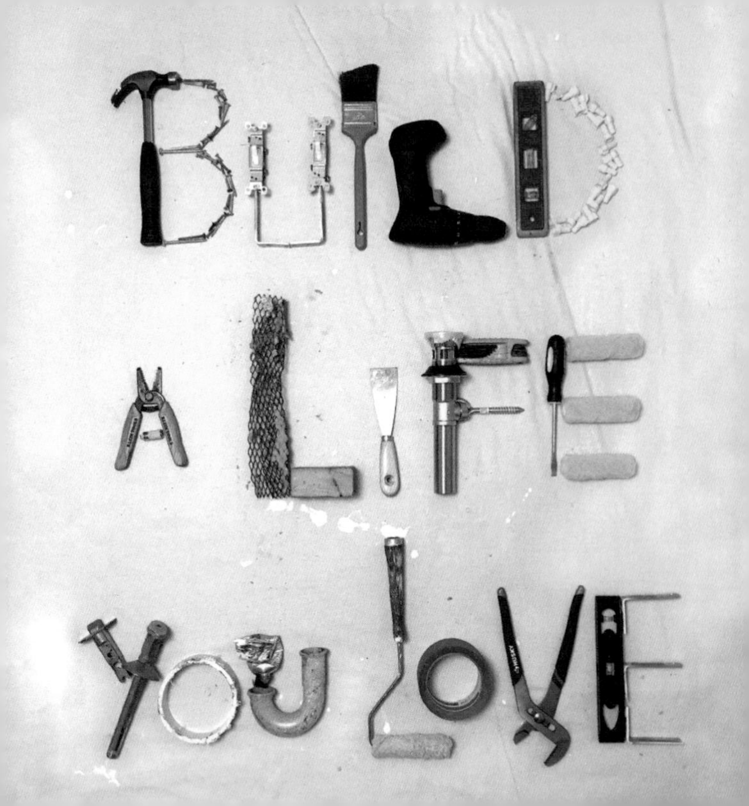
BUILD
A LIFE
YOU LOVE

CARPE THAT DIEM!

TRUST
YOURSELF
COMPLETELY

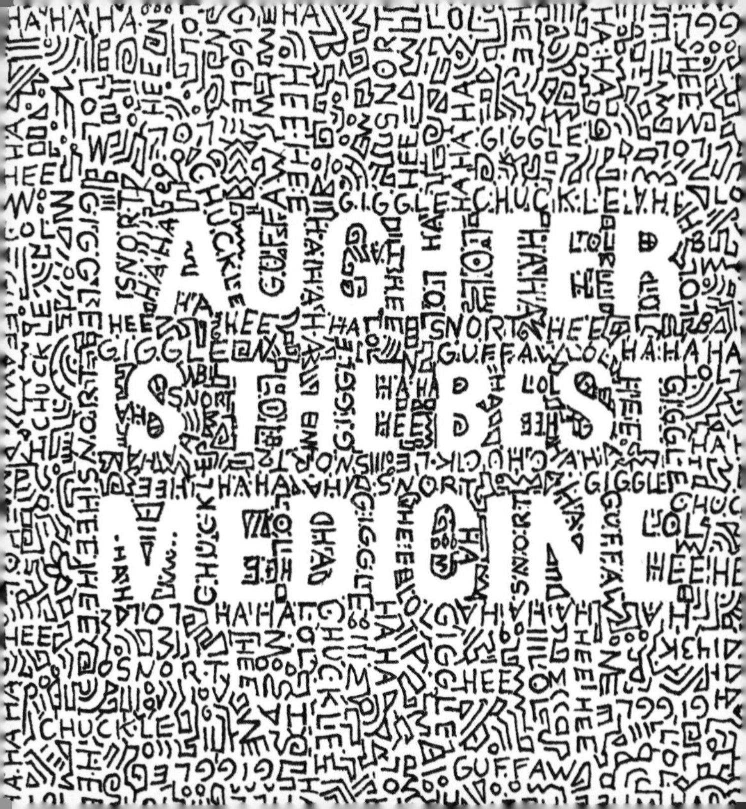
LAUGHTER
IS THE BEST
MEDICINE

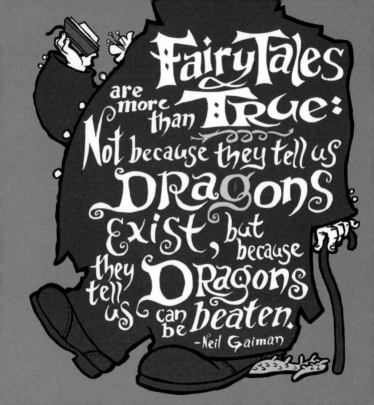

Let Your soul Shine

START YOUR DAY WITH A DANCE PARTY

HOW *WONDERFUL* IT IS THAT NOBODY NEED WAIT A SINGLE MOMENT BEFORE STARTING TO IMPROVE THE WORLD

—ANNE FRANK

INSTANT HAPPY Notes

AND OTHER SURPRISES TO MAKE YOU SMILE

sourcebooks

Copyright © 2017 by Sourcebooks, Inc.
Cover and internal design © 2017 by Sourcebooks, Inc.
Internal artwork by individual artists: John Aardema, Bridget M. Alexander, Elizabeth Boyer, Susan Busch, Catherine Casalino Design, Jennifer K. Beal Davis, Matt Davis, Maggie Edkins, Cassie Gutman, Travis Hasenour, Nicole Hower, Krista Joy Johnson, Kelly Lawler, Michelle McAvoy, Danielle McNaughton, Lin Miceli, Benjamin Nelson, Kay Birkner, Heather Morris, Bethany Orlowski, Ben Ovart, Jenna Quatraro, Jillian Rahn, Kerri Resnick, Kandi Rich, Tina Silva, Becca Sage, Eliza Smith, Allison Sundstrom, Amanda Skolek, Brittany Vibbert, Christine Webster
Internal images © Freepik.com, Unsplash.com, Merfin/GettyImages, sundrawalex/GettyImages, Vit_Mar/GettyImages, Vanzyst/GettyImages, Ukususha/Thinkstock, Julia_Henze/Thinkstock, Vioricalonescu/Thinkstock, speakingtomato/Thinkstock, artJazz/Thinkstock, topform84/Thinkstock, beatpavel/Thinkstock, Martyshova/Thinkstock, yayayoyo/Thinkstock, Lostanastacia/Thinkstock, nata789/Thinkstock, chereshneva/Thinkstock

Published by Sourcebooks, Inc.
P.O. Box 4410, Naperville, Illinois 60567-4410
(630) 961-3900
Fax: (630) 961-2168
www.sourcebooks.com

Printed and bound in China.
LEO 10 9 8 7 6 5 4 3 2 1

A DAY WITHOUT **LAUGHTER** IS A DAY **WASTED**

This collection of notes has been lovingly created by the dreamers, designers, and artists at Sourcebooks for you, our readers. Plus, we were able to include work from a number of friends who share our belief that books change lives. Each unique design is a vision from one of the many people who have the privilege of making books every day. We hope the notes within spark true happiness and create the unique magic only found between the pages of a book.

Thank you

for being a part of our story—now go get happy!

Brittany Vibbert

Meaghan Gibbons

Brittany Vibbert, Art Director

Meaghan Gibbons, Editor

BRIGHTEN UP YOUR DAY

boost the happiness around you with these feel-good notes! You'll find unexpected compliments, much-needed encouragement, lighthearted fun, and silly doodles that are sure to make you grin. The sole purpose of this chunky, compact book is to boost your mood—just think of it as your best friend who will bring you instant happy wherever you go!

THE BEST WAY TO PREDICT THE FUTURE IS TO CREATE IT

—ABRAHAM LINCOLN

NO ONE EXPECTED ME. EVERYTHING AWAITED ME.

—PATTI SMITH

Every Day IS A Fresh START

Light tomorrow with today.

Elizabeth Barrett Browning

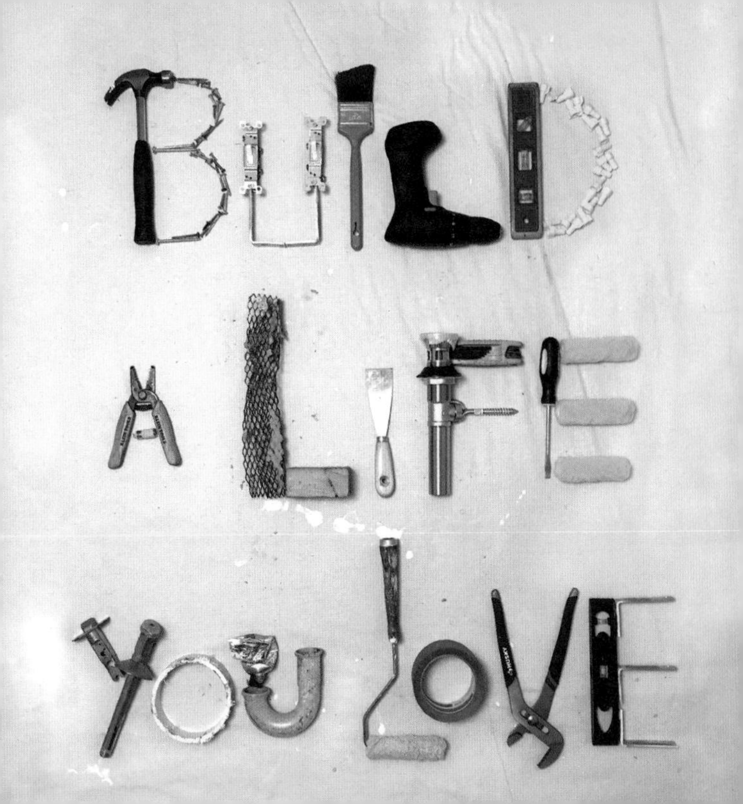
BUILD
A LIFE
YOU LOVE

CARPE THAT DIEM!

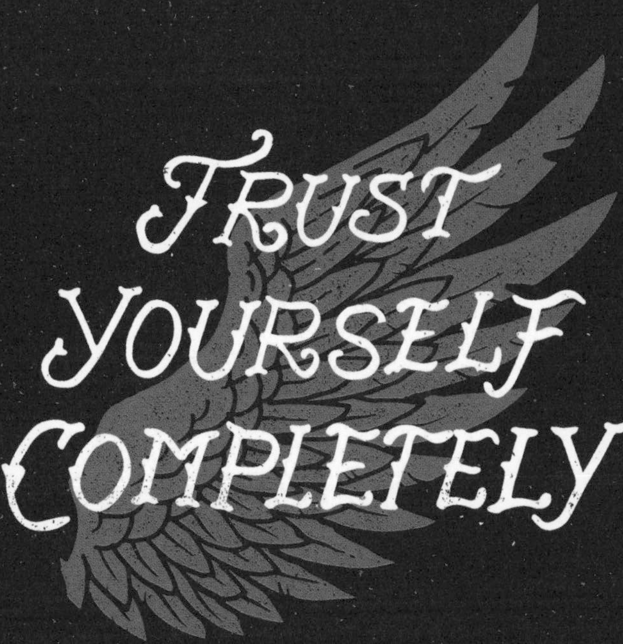
TRUST
YOURSELF
COMPLETELY

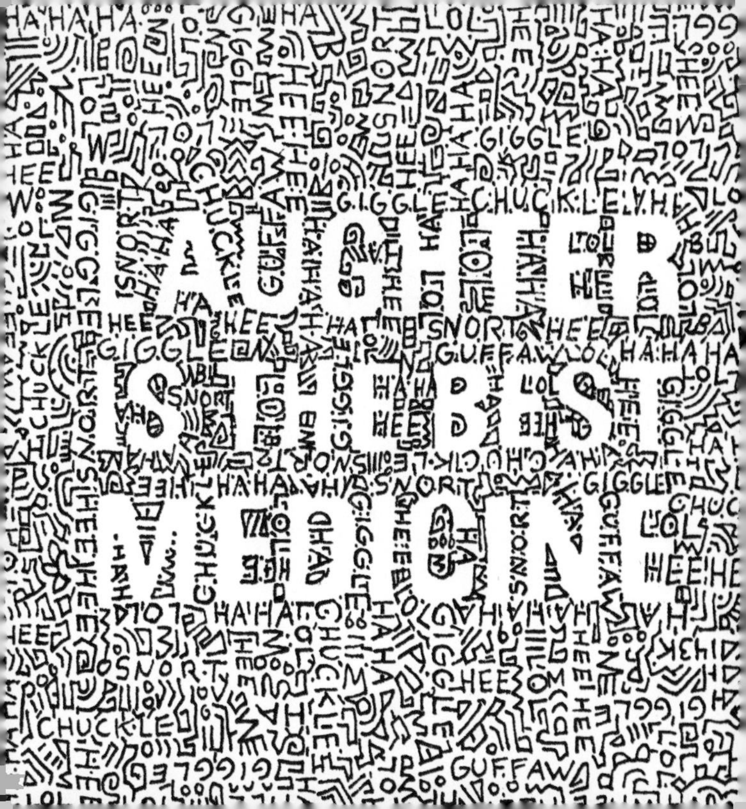
LAUGHTER IS THE BEST MEDICINE

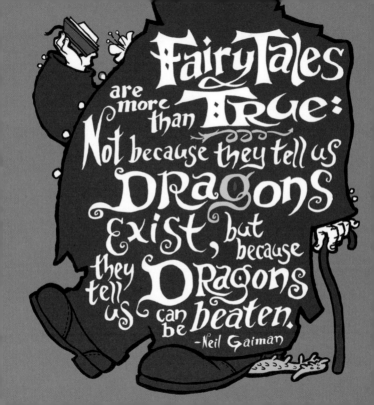

Let Your soul Shine

START YOUR DAY WITH A DANCE PARTY

HOW WONDERFUL IT IS THAT NOBODY NEED WAIT A SINGLE MOMENT BEFORE STARTING TO IMPROVE THE WORLD

—ANNE FRANK

POSITIVE VIBES ONLY :)

HAPPINESS CAN BE FOUND even in the DARKEST TIMES of if one ONLY REMEMBERS to turn on THE LIGHT

—Albus Dumbledore

"the DREAMERS are the SAVIORS of the WORLD"

—JAMES ALLEN

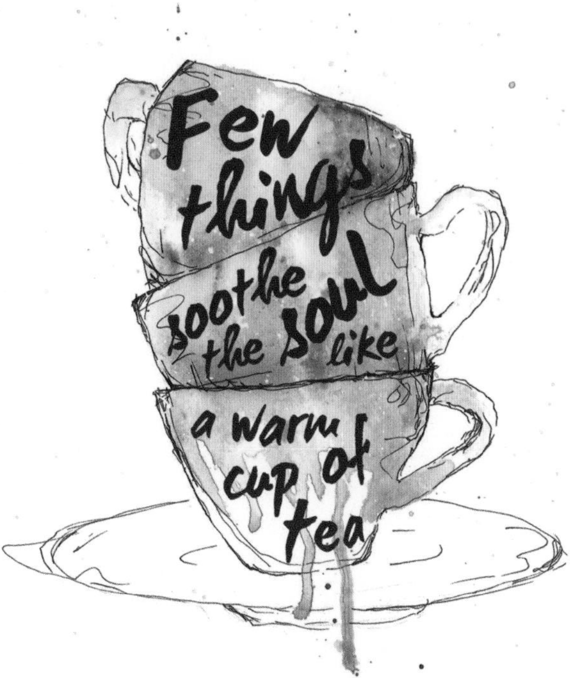
Few things soothe the soul like a warm cup of tea

You put the
Shine
in Sunshine

TO live on purpose,
follow your heart
AND live your
dreams

—MARCIA
WIEDER

THE SUN WILL RISE

getting **LOST** *may be the way* **TO FIND YOURSELF**

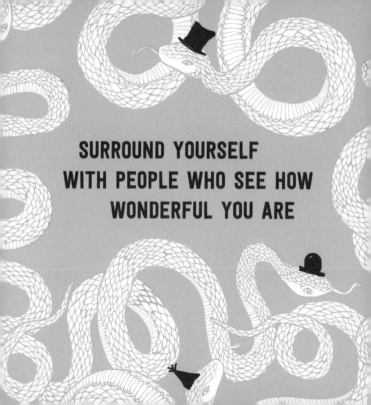

SURROUND YOURSELF
WITH PEOPLE WHO SEE HOW
WONDERFUL YOU ARE

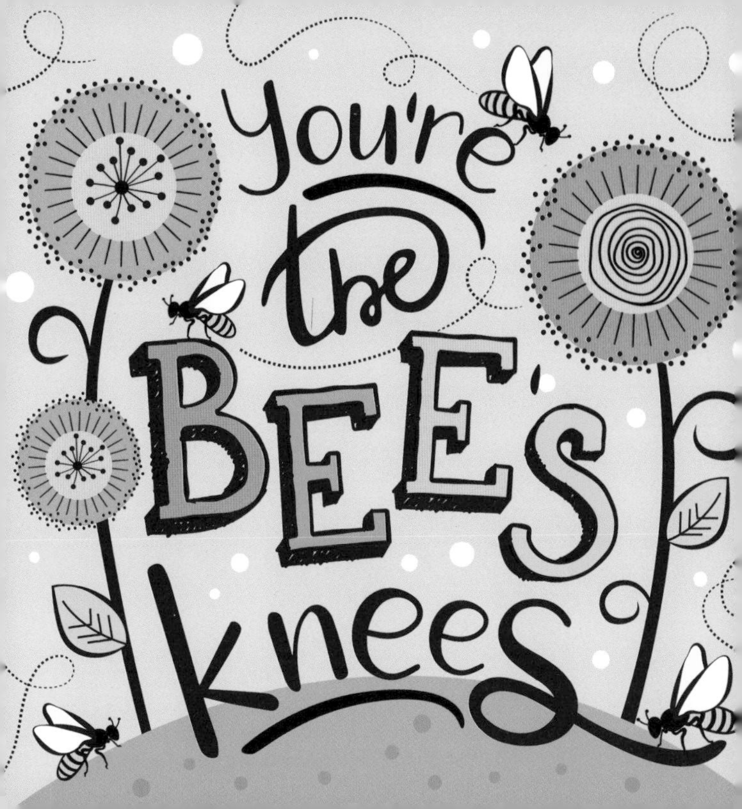
You're the BEE'S knees

TODAY YOU ARE YOU,
THAT IS TRUER THAN TRUE.
THERE IS NO ONE ALIVE
WHO IS YOUER THAN YOU.

~DR. SEUSS, *HAPPY BIRTHDAY TO YOU!*

STAY *gold*

—THE OUTSIDERS

BELIEVE IN YOURSELF

PREPARE ACCORDINGLY.

WHO IS THE *happier* MAN?
HE WHO **BRAVED** THE
Storm OF *Life*
AND **LIVED**–OR HE **WHO**
STAYED SECURELY ON
Shore AND MERELY
EXISTED?

Hunter S. Thompson

KID, YOU'LL MOVE MOUNTAINS! today is your day! YOUR MOUNTAIN IS WAITING. so get on your way!

— Dr. Seuss

DANCE to your
OWN RHYTHM

Kill THEM with kindness

GREAT THINGS

ARE JUST

THE CORNER

ONE SMALL ACT
OF KINDNESS CAN
CHANGE THE WORLD

MAKE AN EFFORT
to feel
PROUD
of yourself
TODAY

Throw kindness around like

confetti

add a little
EXTRA
to your
ORDINARY

Let the world see you SHINE

LET'S FIND A PLACE TO GET LOST

Wave your SMILE as your own personal flag

you make me
happy
when skies
are gray

BREAK OUT

OF YOUR

COMFORT ZONE

It's a
good day
to have a
good day

YOU ARE MORE THAN Good Enough

YOUR THINKING

CHANGE

YOUR LIFE

Be truthful, gentle, and

FEARLESS.

—Mahatma Gandhi

love is that condition in which the **happiness** of another person is essential to your own

– ROBERT HEINLEIN –

LIFE *was meant to be* **LIVED**, & CURIOSITY MUST BE KEPT ALIVE. ONE MUST NEVER, *for whatever reason,* TURN HIS BACK ON **LIFE**.

· ELEANOR ROOSEVELT ·

No man is lonely while eating

SPAGHETTI

— Christopher Morley

Those
who bring
sunshine
into the lives of others cannot
keep it from themselves.

—J. M. Barrie

BIG THINGS often come from SMALL BEGINNINGS

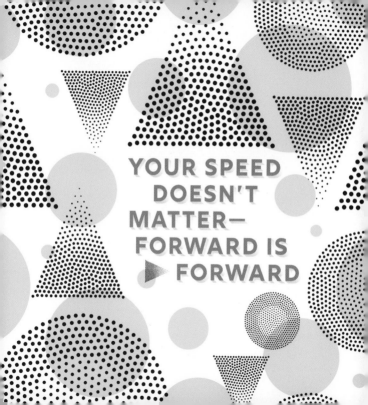

YOUR SPEED DOESN'T MATTER— FORWARD IS ▶ FORWARD

SOMETIMES YOU NEED TO SINK ALL THE WAY TO THE BOTTOM OF THE POOL TO SHOOT OUT OF THE WATER

DOUBT

KILLS

MORE

dreams

THAN

FAILURE

EVER

WILL

—SUZY KASSEM

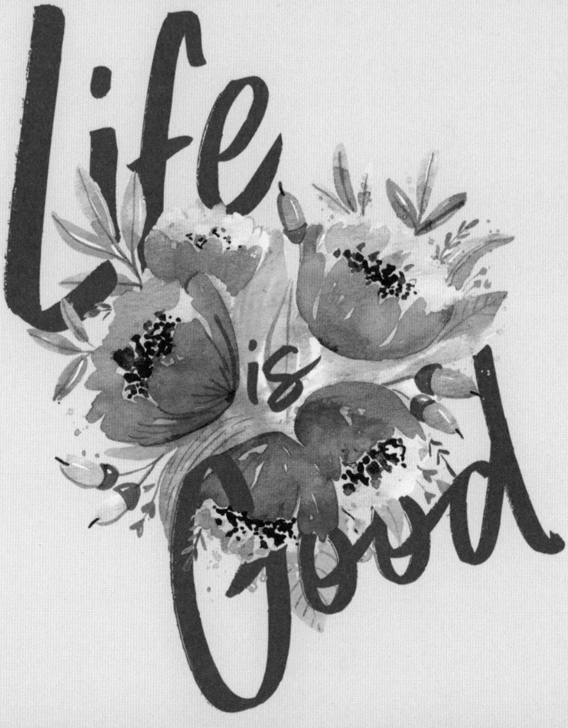
Life
is
Good

LIFE IS EITHER

A DARING ADVENTURE OR NOTHING

—HELEN KELLER

I URGE YOU TO PLEASE NOTICE WHEN
· *You are happy* ·
+ EXCLAIM —————
————— *or* MURMUR —————
————— *or* THINK
· AT SOME POINT, "IF THIS ISN'T NICE, ·
I don't know what is.

KURT VONNEGUT

LIFE MIGHT NOT ALWAYS BE *perfect*, BUT IF *you look* HARD ENOUGH, YOU WILL SEE IT IS ALWAYS *magical*

BE SOMEONE'S

★

HERO

★ ★ ★

There is no
Beauty
without some
Strangeness

— Edgar Allan Poe

Be happy
for this moment.
This moment
is your life.

C'est La Vie

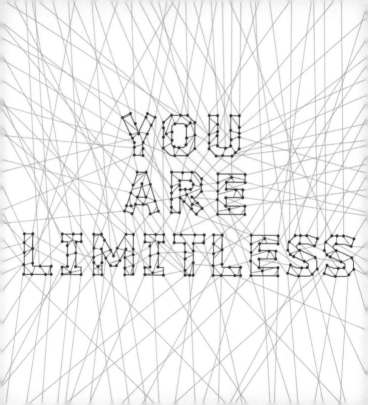

DON'T STOP UNTIL YOU'RE PROUD

there can't be
flowers
without rain

Life

moves pretty fast. If you don't **STOP** and **look** around once in awhile, you could **miss it.**

-ferris Bueller

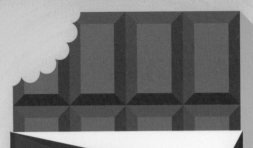

NOTHING TURNS A
BAD MOOD
INTO A *good one*
FASTER THAN
CHOCOLATE

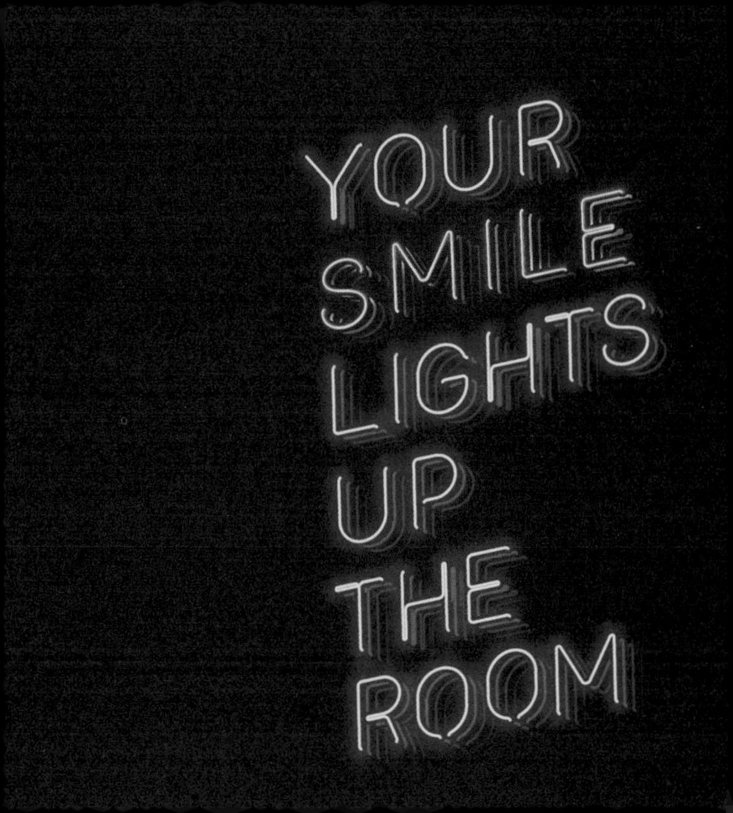
YOUR
SMILE
LIGHTS
UP
THE
ROOM

THE
SWEETEST *joy,*

THE WILDEST WOE IS

LOVE.

—PEARL
BAILEY

I'd far rather be happy than right any day.

Douglas Adams

If you spend too much time
searching for the perfect life,
you might miss the fact
that you already have one

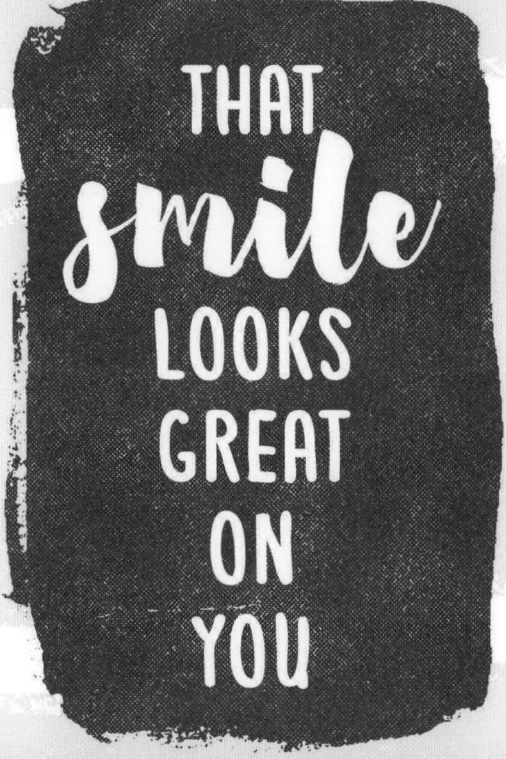
THAT
smile
LOOKS
GREAT
ON
YOU

"BEAUTY IS IN THE EYE OF THE BEHOLDER AND IT MAY BE NECESSARY FROM TIME TO TIME TO GIVE A STUPID OR MISINFORMED BEHOLDER A BLACK EYE."

—MISS PIGGY

Every day is the PERFECT DAY to BINGE WATCH a season OF YOUR FAVORITE show

THROW YOUR PARTY PANTS ON!

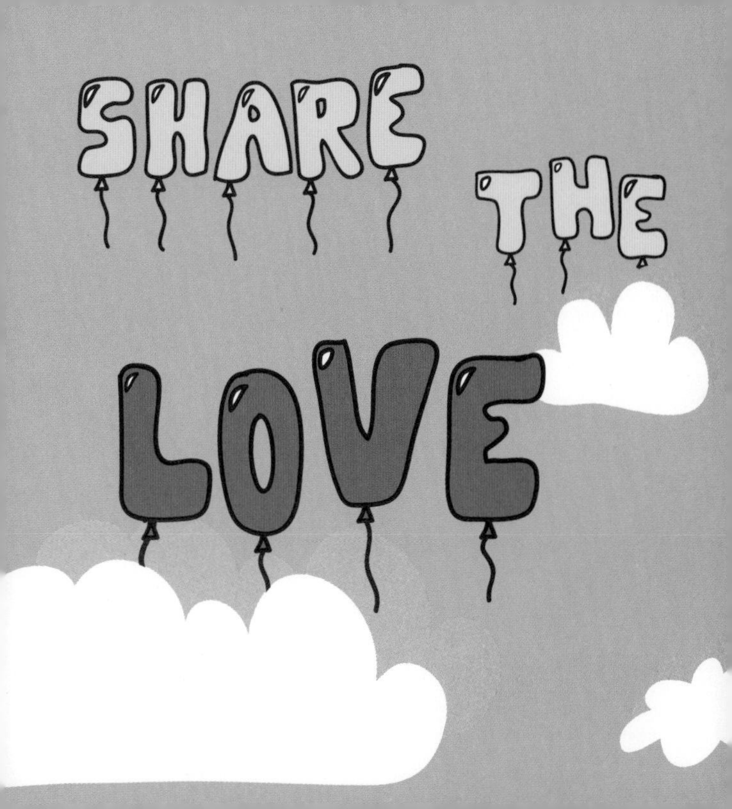
SHARE THE
LOVE

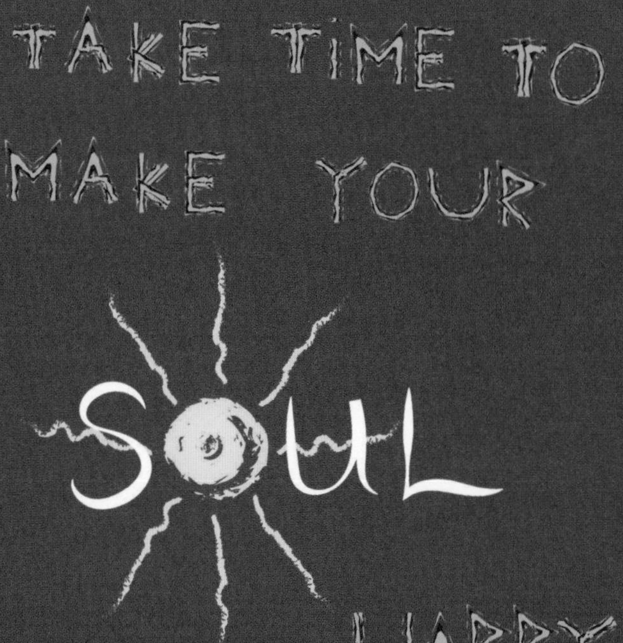
TAKE TIME TO
MAKE YOUR
SOUL
HAPPY

strive to be

present

in every aspect

of your life

ALWAYS LOOK FOR THE GOOD IN PEOPLE

collect new
experiences

friendship
isn't a
big thing
—
it's a
million little
things

—anonymous

all You need is ICE CREAM

DARE TO LIVE
THE LIFE YOU HAVE
DREAMED FOR YOURSELF.
GO FORWARD AND MAKE
YOUR DREAMS COME TRUE.

—RALPH WALDO EMERSON

be BOLD

A good laugh
and a long sleep
are the two best
CURES FOR ANYTHING

IRISH PROVERB

YOU'RE A *Real* GEM

I THINK IF YOU CAN DANCE AND BE FREE
AND NOT EMBARRASSED, YOU CAN RULE THE WORLD

—AMY POEHLER

you are
loved

TREAT YOURSELF
to an ice cream
sundae:
something about
SPRINKLES, Hot Fudge,
& whipped cream
CAN MAKE ANYONE
smile.

MAKE SILLY FACES.
THEY WON'T STAY
LIKE THAT FOREVER,
NO MATTER WHAT YOUR
MOTHER TOLD YOU.

Hello, SUNSHINE!

happiness is a habit

IF YOU STUMBLE,
MAKE IT PART
OF THE DANCE

TAKE A MOMENT AND
THINK ABOUT ALL YOU HAVE.
JOY STARTS WITH A GRATEFUL

MAKE TODAY AMAZING

ONCE YOU CHOOSE

hope,

ANYTHING

IS

Possible

—CHRISTOPHER REEVE

BE SILLY.
BE HONEST.
BE KIND.

—RALPH WALDO EMERSON

decisions

DETERMINE

destiny

Happiness is not a state to arrive at but a manner of traveling.

EVERY DAY IS
AN OPPORTUNITY TO
LEARN SOMETHING NEW

sMILES

ARE ALWAYS TRENDING

Happiness IS NOT A destination. IT IS A method of life

— BURTON HILLS

IN A WORLD WHERE YOU CAN BE ANYTHING

be kind.

YOU ARE THE UNDISPUTED WORLD CHAMPION OF BEING YOU

A LITTLE MAGIC

CAN TAKE YOU A LONG WAY

-ROALD DAHL

Cherish
THE
SIMPLE THINGS

Beautiful Minds Inspire others

The future belongs to
those who believe in the

Beauty
of their
Dreams

—Eleanor
Roosevelt

if more
of us VALUED
FOOD and CHEER
& Song ABOVE
HOARDED GOLD,
it would be
A MERRIER WORLD.

J. R. R. Tolkien

IF there IS NO STRUGGLE, THERE IS NO PROGRESS

Frederick Douglass

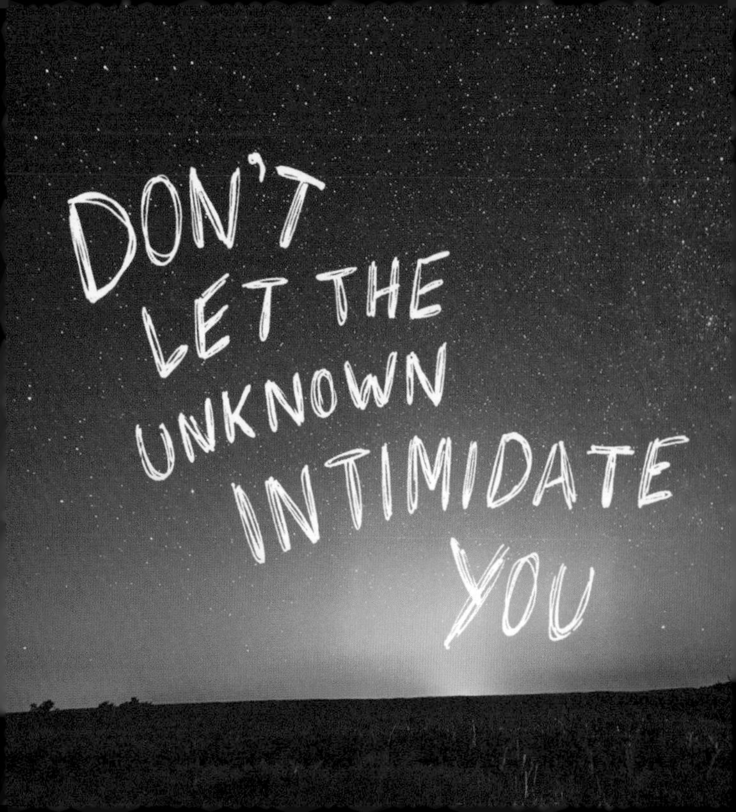
DON'T
LET THE
UNKNOWN
INTIMIDATE
YOU

YOU have to go a little **CRAZY** every once in a while to stay **SANE**

You

you're a

natural

do **you.**

at it.

take some time to
catch up with an old friend

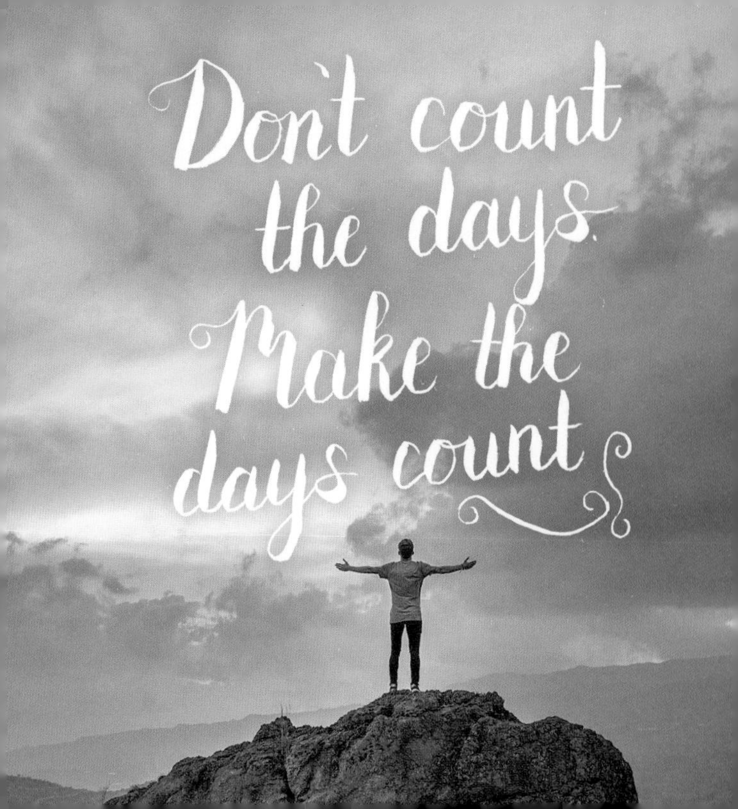
Don't count the days.
Make the days count.

Creativity is intelligence HAVING fun

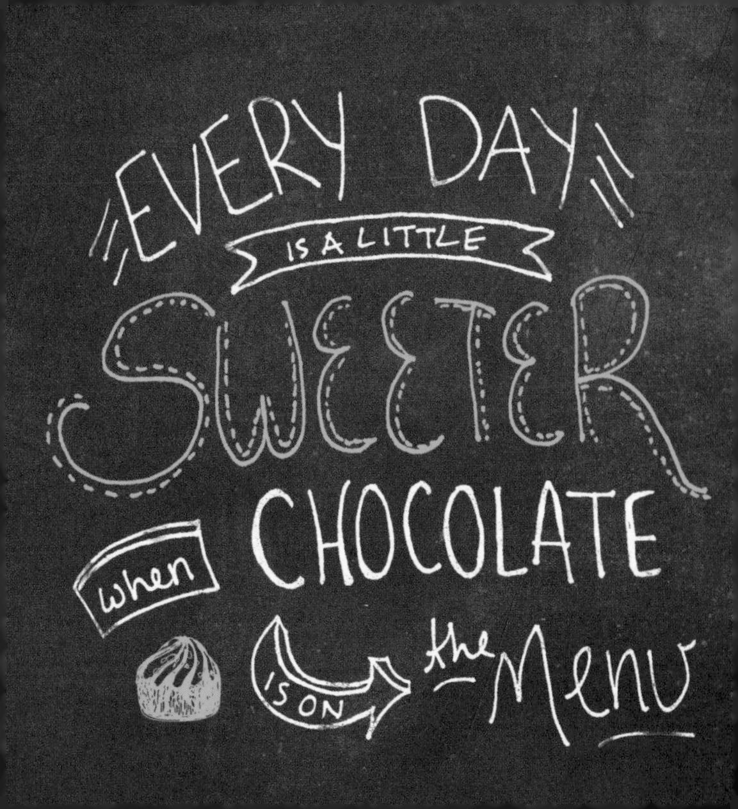
EVERY DAY
IS A LITTLE
SWEETER
when
CHOCOLATE
IS ON
the Menu

LIFE IS TOO
SHORT
TO NOT
EXPRESS
YOURSELF

MAKE SOMEONE ELSE HAPPY,
AND YOUR OWN HAPPINESS
WILL WORK ITSELF OUT

LIFE IS TOO SHORT TO BE bored

you are SERIOUSLY GREAT

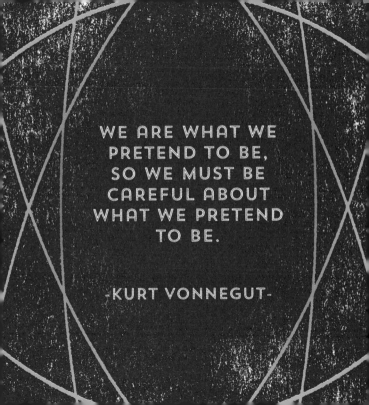

the only

DIFFERENCE *between*

DRAMA

&

COMEDY

is PERSPECTIVE

Be your own you!

be a flamingo in a flock of pigeons

be a
GOOFBALL
every once in a while

live. LAUGH. LOVE. (REPEAT.)

LIFE ISN'T ABOUT FINDING YOURSELF.
LIFE IS ABOUT CREATING YOURSELF.

—GEORGE BERNARD SHAW—

take time to SMELL the Roses

you are BRAVER than you BELIEVE, STRONGER than you SEEM, and SMARTER than you THINK.

—A. A. Milne, *Winnie-the-Pooh*

PEOPLE WHO
love TO EAT
ARE THE
BEST PEOPLE

—JULIA CHILD

time you enjoy wasting is not wasted time

MARTHE TROLY-CURTIN

GRIN
and
SHARE IT

LET SOMEONE KNOW
YOU LOVE THEM,
EVEN IF THAT
SOMEONE
IS YOURSELF

THE WORLD IS A BETTER PLACE BECAUSE YOU'RE IN IT

INSTANT HAPPY

Notes

AND OTHER SURPRISES TO MAKE YOU SMILE

sourcebooks

Published by Sourcebooks, Inc.
P.O. Box 4410, Naperville, Illinois 60567-4410
(630) 961-3900
Fax: (630) 961-2168
www.sourcebooks.com

Printed and bound in China.
LEO 10 9 8 7 6 5 4 3 2 1

A DAY WITHOUT

LAUGHTER

IS A DAY

WASTED

This collection of notes has been lovingly created by the dreamers, designers, and artists at Sourcebooks for you, our readers. Plus, we were able to include work from a number of friends who share our belief that books change lives. Each unique design is a vision from one of the many people who have the privilege of making books every day. We hope the notes within spark true happiness and create the unique magic only found between the pages of a book.

Thank you

for being a part of our story—now go get happy!

Brittany Vibbert, Art Director

Meaghan Gibbons, Editor

BRIGHTEN UP YOUR DAY

boost the happiness around you with these feel-good notes! You'll find unexpected compliments, much-needed encouragement, lighthearted fun, and silly doodles that are sure to make you grin. The sole purpose of this chunky, compact book is to boost your mood—just think of it as your best friend who will bring you instant happy wherever you go!

THE BEST WAY TO PREDICT THE FUTURE IS TO CREATE IT

-ABRAHAM LINCOLN

Let go, move forward.

Every Day is a Fresh Start

INSTANT HAPPY

Notes

AND OTHER SURPRISES TO MAKE YOU SMILE

sourcebooks

Copyright © 2017 by Sourcebooks, Inc.
Cover and internal design © 2017 by Sourcebooks, Inc.
Internal artwork by individual artists: John Aardema, Bridget M. Alexander, Elizabeth Boyer, Susan Busch, Catherine Casalino Design, Jennifer K. Beal Davis, Matt Davis, Maggie Edkins, Cassie Gutman, Travis Hasenour, Nicole Hower, Krista Joy Johnson, Kelly Lawler, Michelle McAvoy, Danielle McNaughton, Lin Miceli, Benjamin Nelson, Kay Birkner, Heather Morris, Bethany Orlowski, Ben Ouart, Jenna Quatraro, Jillian Rahn, Kerri Resnick, Kandi Rich, Tina Silva, Becca Sage, Eliza Smith, Allison Sundstrom, Amanda Skolek, Brittany Vibbert, Christine Webster
Internal images © Freepik.com, Unsplash.com, Merfin/GettyImages, sundrawalex/GettyImages, Vit_Mar/GettyImages, Vanzyst/GettyImages, Ukususha/Thinkstock, Julia_Henze/Thinkstock, Vioricalonescu/Thinkstock, speakingtomato/Thinkstock, artJazz/Thinkstock, topform84/Thinkstock, beatpavel/Thinkstock, Martyshova/Thinkstock, yayayoyo/Thinkstock, Lostanastacia/Thinkstock, nata789/Thinkstock, chereshneva/Thinkstock

Sourcebooks and the colophon are registered trademarks of Sourcebooks, Inc.

Published by Sourcebooks, Inc.
P.O. Box 4410, Naperville, Illinois 60567-4410
(630) 961-3900
Fax: (630) 961-2168
www.sourcebooks.com

Printed and bound in China.
EO 10 9 8 7 6 5 4 3 2 1

A DAY WITHOUT

LAUGHTER

IS A DAY

WASTED

This collection of notes has been lovingly created by the dreamers, designers, and artists at Sourcebooks for you, our readers. Plus, we were able to include work from a number of friends who share our belief that books change lives. Each unique design is a vision from one of the many people who have the privilege of making books every day. We hope the notes within spark true happiness and create the unique magic only found between the pages of a book.

Thank you

for being a part of our story—now go get happy!

Brittany Vibbert

Brittany Vibbert, Art Director

Meaghan Gibbons

Meaghan Gibbons, Editor

BRIGHTEN

UP

YOUR

DAY

boost the happiness around you with these feel-good notes! You'll find unexpected compliments, much-needed encouragement, lighthearted fun, and silly doodles that are sure to make you grin. The sole purpose of this chunky, compact book is to boost your mood—just think of it as your best friend who will bring you instant happy wherever you go!

TAKE THE Scenic route

THE BEST WAY TO PREDICT THE FUTURE IS TO CREATE IT
— ABRAHAM LINCOLN

Let go, move forward.

NOTHING ME.
EXPECTED ME.
EVERYTHING
ME.
AWAITED ME. —PATTI SMITH

Every Day IS A Fresh START

Light tomorrow with today.

Elizabeth Barrett Browning

BUILD A LIFE YOU LOVE

IT'S OK TO TAKE A BREAK

CARPE THAT DIEM!

TRUST
YOURSELF
COMPLETELY

LAUGHTER IS THE BEST MEDICINE

Let Your soul Shine

START YOUR DAY WITH A DANCE PARTY

HOW **WONDERFUL** IT IS THAT NOBODY NEED WAIT A SINGLE MOMENT BEFORE STARTING TO IMPROVE THE WORLD

—ANNE FRANK

POSITIVE VIBES ONLY :)

HAPPINESS CAN BE FOUND even in the DARKEST TIMES of if one ONLY REMEMBERS to turn on THE LIGHT

—Albus Dumbledore

"the DREAMERS are the SAVIORS of the WORLD"

—JAMES ALLEN

Few things soothe the soul like a warm cup of tea

You
put the
Shine
in
Sunshine

TO live on purpose,
follow your heart
AND live your
dreams

—MARCIA
WIEDER

IT'S
COMFORT
FOOD
O'CLOCK

getting **LOST** may be the way **TO FIND** YOURSELF

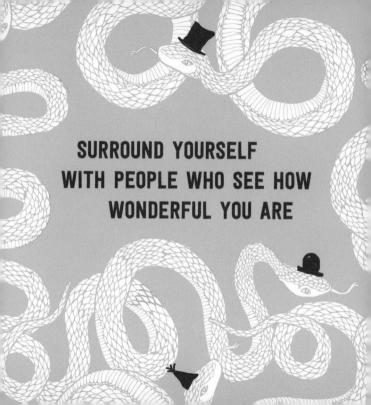

SURROUND YOURSELF
WITH PEOPLE WHO SEE HOW
WONDERFUL YOU ARE

TODAY YOU ARE YOU,

THAT IS TRUER THAN TRUE.

THERE IS NO ONE ALIVE

WHO IS YOUER THAN YOU.

~DR. SEUSS, HAPPY BIRTHDAY TO YOU!

STAY *gold*

—THE OUTSIDERS

BELIEVE IN YOURSELF

EAT SOME CHOCOLATE CAKE TODAY!

PREPARE ACCORDINGLY.

WHO IS THE *happier* MAN?
HE WHO **BRAVED** THE
Storm OF *Life*
AND **LIVED**—OR HE **WHO**
STAYED SECURELY ON
Shore AND MERELY
EXISTED?

~~~~~~~~

Hunter S. Thompson

KID, YOU'LL MOVE MOUNTAINS!
today is your day!
YOUR MOUNTAIN
IS WAITING.
so get on your way!

— Dr. Seuss

Lose
yourself
in a great
book

DANCE to your OWN RHYTHM

Kill THEM *with* **kindness**

GREAT THINGS ARE JUST THE CORNER

ONE SMALL ACT
OF KINDNESS CAN
CHANGE THE WORLD

MAKE AN EFFORT
to feel
PROUD
of yourself
TODAY

Throw kindness around like

confetti

add a little
EXTRA
to your
ORDINARY

Let the world see you SHINE

LET'S FIND A PLACE TO GET LOST

Wave your SMILE as your own personal flag

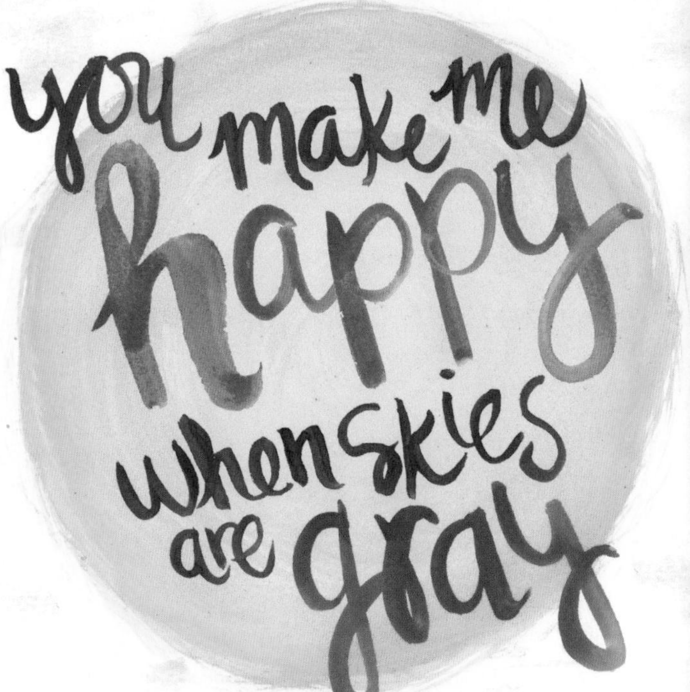
you make me
happy
when skies
are gray

It's a good day to have a good day

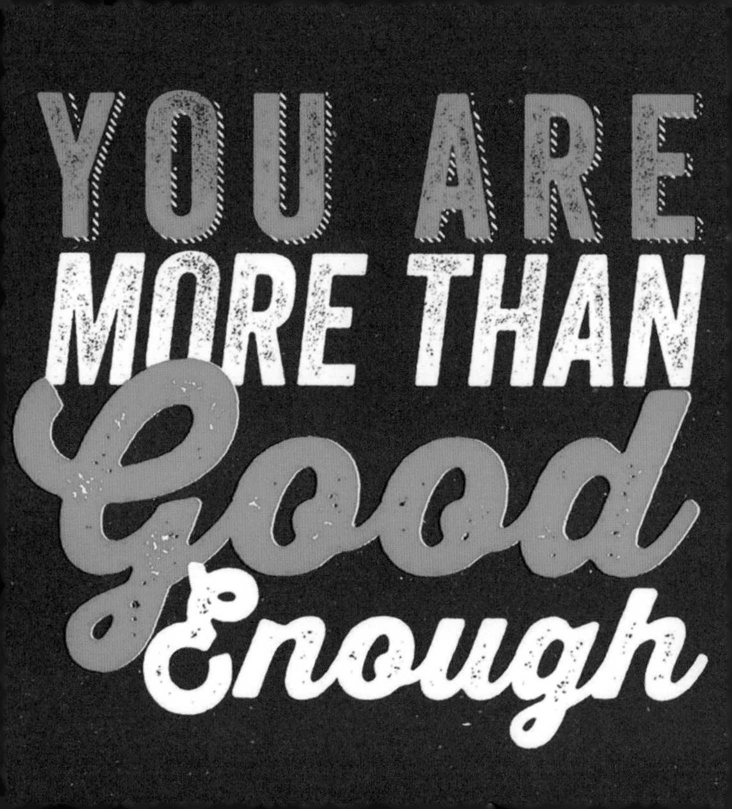
YOU ARE
MORE THAN
Good
Enough

A little
kindness
can go
a long
way

YOUR THINKING
CHANGE
YOUR LIFE

Be truthful, gentle, and

FEARLESS.

—Mahatma Gandhi

love is that condition in which the **happiness** of another person is essential to your own

– ROBERT HEINLEIN –

LIFE

was meant to be

LIVED, & CURIOSITY

MUST BE KEPT ALIVE.

ONE MUST NEVER,

for whatever reason,

TURN HIS BACK

ON LIFE.

· ELEANOR ROOSEVELT ·

No man is lonely while eating

SPAGHETTI

— Christopher Morley

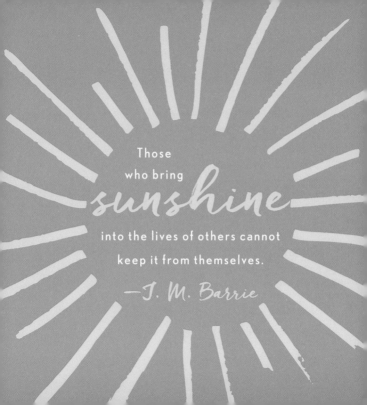

Those
who bring
sunshine
into the lives of others cannot
keep it from themselves.

—J. M. Barrie

BIG THINGS often come from SMALL BEGINNINGS

YOUR SPEED DOESN'T MATTER— FORWARD IS FORWARD

SOMETIMES YOU NEED TO SINK ALL THE WAY TO THE BOTTOM OF THE POOL TO SHOOT OUT OF THE WATER

DOUBT

KILLS

MORE

dreams

THAN

FAILURE

EVER

WILL

—suzy kassem

LIFE IS EITHER

A DARING ADVENTURE OR NOTHING

—HELEN KELLER

I URGE YOU TO PLEASE NOTICE WHEN *You are happy* + EXCLAIM or MURMUR or THINK

• AT SOME POINT, "IF THIS ISN'T NICE, • *I don't know what is.*"

KURT VONNEGUT

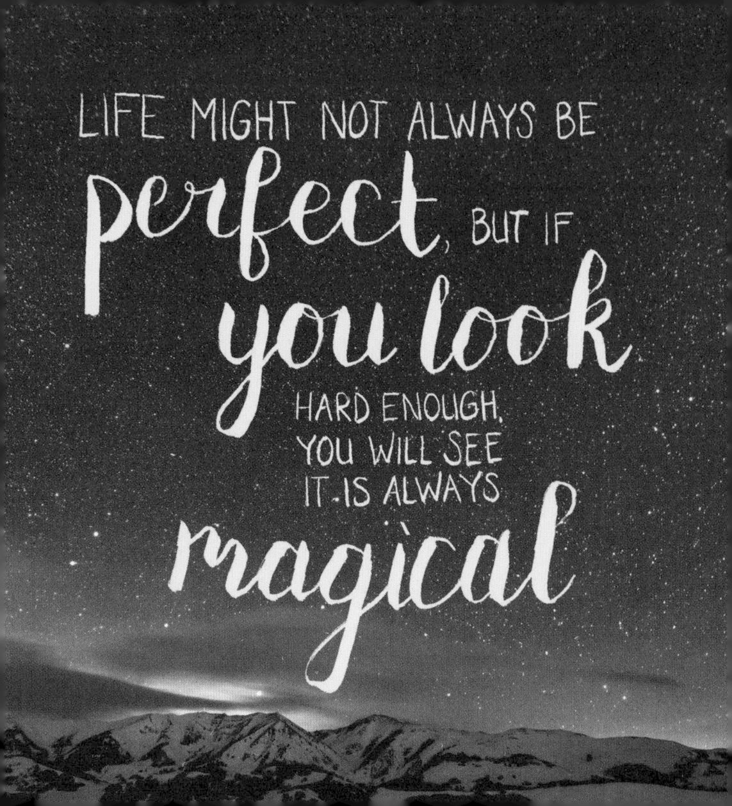
LIFE MIGHT NOT ALWAYS BE
perfect, BUT IF
you look
HARD ENOUGH,
YOU WILL SEE
IT IS ALWAYS
magical

BE SOMEONE'S HERO

There is no **Beauty** without some **Strangeness**

— Edgar Allan Poe

Be happy
for this moment.
This moment
is your life.

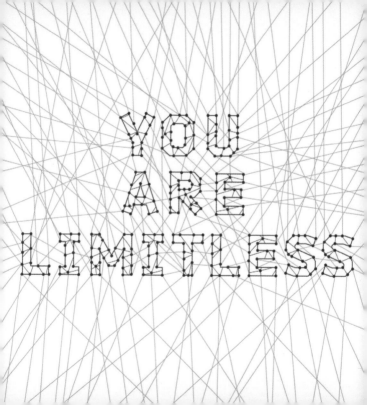

DON'T STOP UNTIL YOU'RE PROUD

there can't be
flowers
without rain

Life

moves pretty fast.
If you don't STOP and
look around
once in awhile,
you could

miss
it.

-ferris Bueller

NOTHING TURNS A
BAD MOOD
INTO A *good one*
FASTER THAN
CHOCOLATE

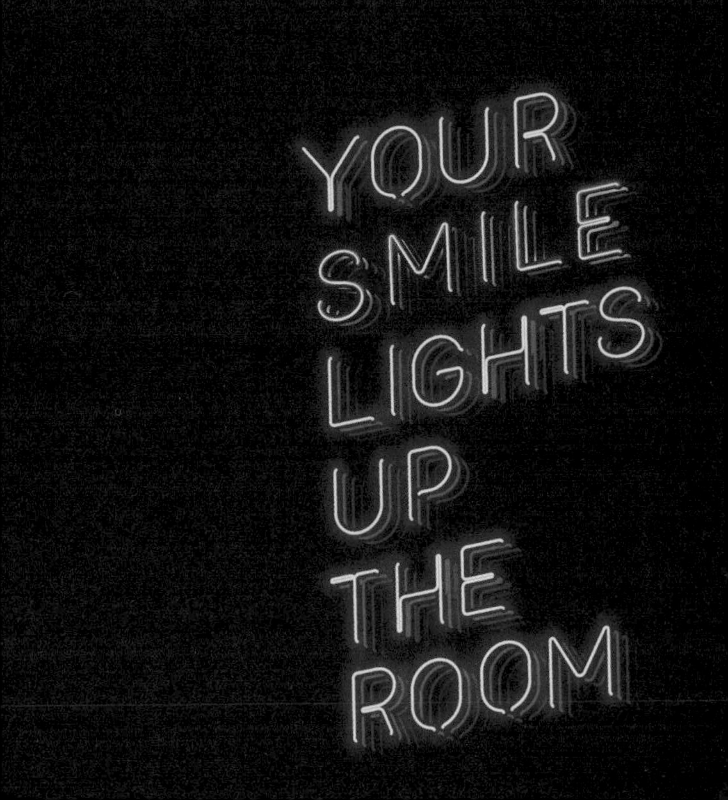
YOUR
SMILE
LIGHTS
UP
THE
ROOM

THE
SWEETEST *joy*,

THE WILDEST WOE IS

LOVE.

—PEARL
BAILEY

ONLY GET DOWN
ON THE
DANCE FLOOR

I'd far rather be happy than right any day.

Douglas Adams

If you spend too much time
searching for the perfect life,
you might miss the fact
that you already have one

compliment
a stranger

THAT *smile* LOOKS GREAT ON YOU

"BEAUTY IS IN THE EYE OF THE BEHOLDER AND IT MAY BE NECESSARY FROM TIME TO TIME TO GIVE A STUPID OR MISINFORMED BEHOLDER A BLACK EYE."

—MISS PIGGY

Every day is the PERFECT DAY to BINGE WATCH a season OF YOUR FAVORITE show

THROW YOUR

PRTY

PANTS

→ON!←

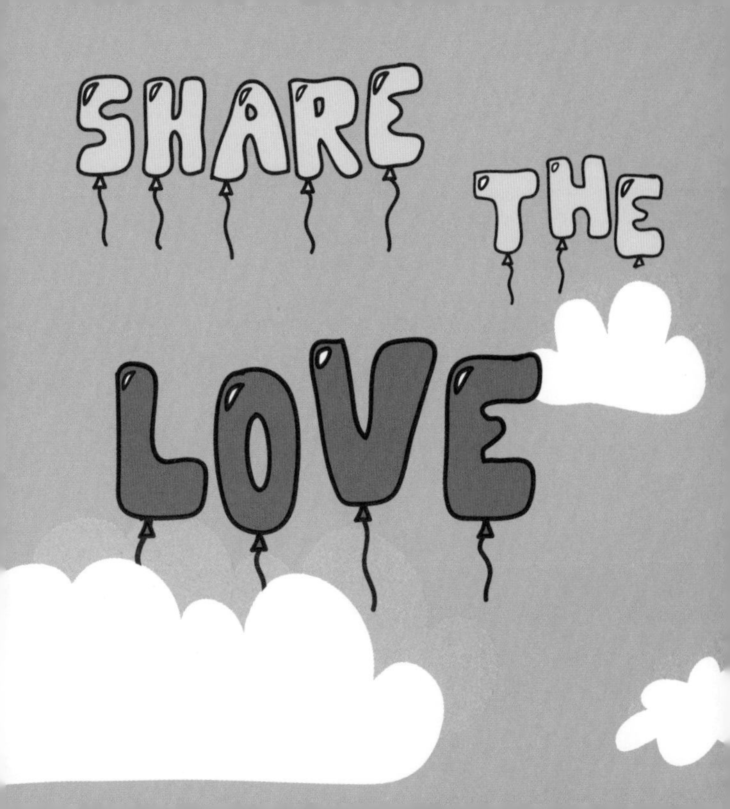
SHARE THE
LOVE

TAKE TIME TO MAKE YOUR

SOUL

HAPPY

strive to be

present

in every aspect

of your life

ALWAYS LOOK FOR THE GOOD IN PEOPLE

collect new
experiences

friendship
isn't a
big thing
—
it's a
million little
things

-anonymous

all You need is ICE CREAM

The Official ANIMAL of Scotland is the Unicorn

DARE TO LIVE
THE LIFE YOU HAVE
DREAMED FOR YOURSELF.
GO FORWARD AND MAKE
YOUR DREAMS COME TRUE.

—RALPH WALDO EMERSON

be

BOLD

A good **laugh**
and a long **sleep**
are the two best
CURES FOR **ANYTHING**

IRISH PROVERB

YOU'RE A

Real

GEM

I THINK IF YOU CAN DANCE AND BE FREE
AND NOT EMBARRASSED, YOU CAN RULE THE WORLD

—AMY POEHLER

you are loved

TREAT YOURSELF
to an ice cream
sundae:
something about
SPRINKLES, Hot Fudge,
& whipped cream
CAN MAKE ANYONE
smile:

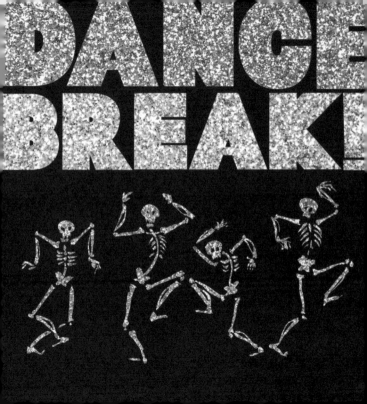

MAKE SILLY FACES.
THEY WON'T STAY
LIKE THAT FOREVER,
NO MATTER WHAT YOUR
MOTHER TOLD YOU.

happiness is a habit

IF YOU STUMBLE, MAKE IT PART OF THE DANCE

TAKE A MOMENT AND THINK ABOUT ALL YOU HAVE. JOY STARTS WITH A GRATEFUL

HEART

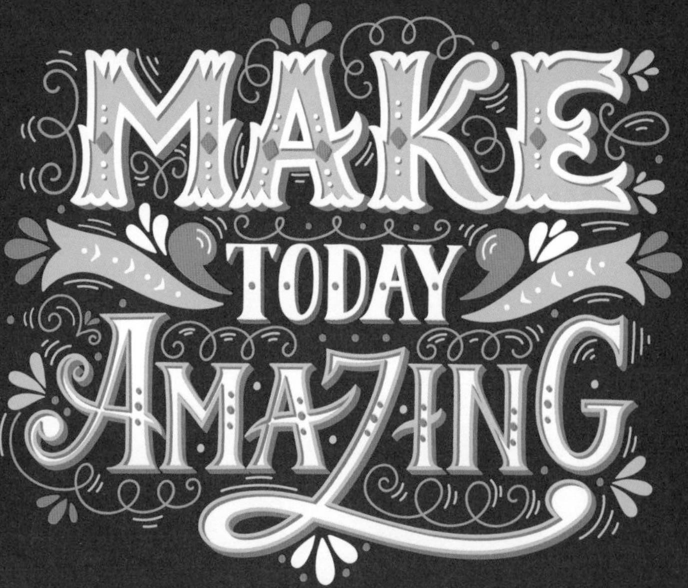
MAKE
TODAY
AMAZING

ONCE YOU CHOOSE

hope,

ANYTHING

IS

Possible

—CHRISTOPHER REEVE

BE SILLY.
BE HONEST.
BE KIND.

—RALPH WALDO EMERSON

decisions

DETERMINE

destiny

Happiness is not a state to arrive at but a manner of traveling.

EVERY DAY IS
AN OPPORTUNITY TO
LEARN SOMETHING NEW

sMILES

ARE ALWAYS TRENDING

Happiness is not a destination. It is a method of life.

— Burton Hills

In a world where you can be anything, be kind.

YOU ARE THE UNDISPUTED WORLD CHAMPION OF BEING YOU

Be WHO YOU WERE Born TO Be

A LITTLE
MAGIC
CAN TAKE YOU A LONG WAY

-ROALD DAHL

Cherish the simple things

Beautiful Minds Inspire Others

The future belongs to those who believe in the *Beauty of their Dreams*

—Eleanor Roosevelt

if more
of us VALUED
FOOD and CHEER
& Song ABOVE
HOARDED GOLD,
it would be
A MERRIER WORLD.

J. R. R. Tolkien

IF there is NO STRUGGLE, THERE is NO PROGRESS

Frederick Douglass

give
yourself
a
break

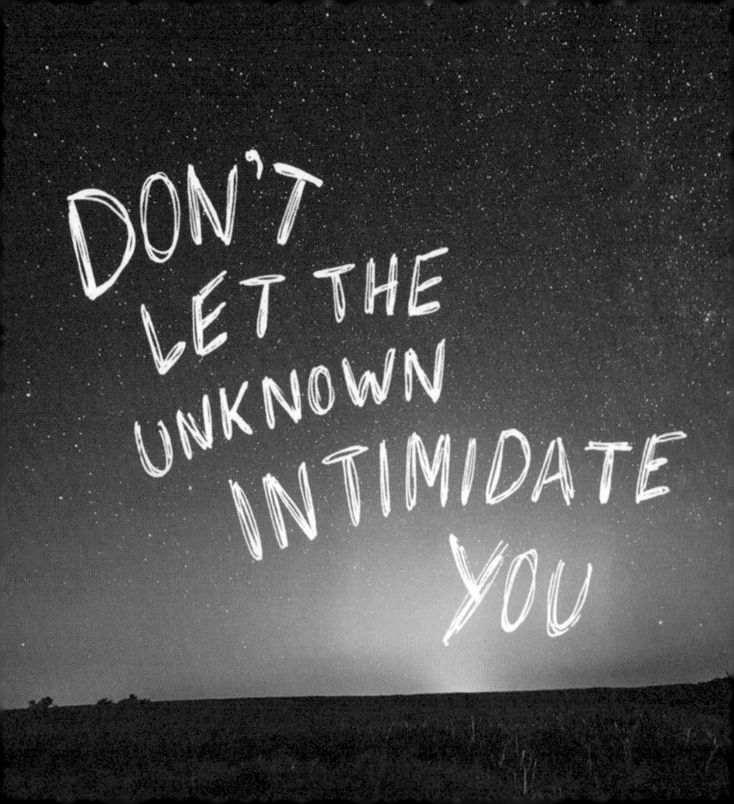
DON'T
LET THE
UNKNOWN
INTIMIDATE
YOU

YOU have to go a little **CRAZY** every once in a while to stay **SANE**

You do you.

You're a natural at it.

take some time to
catch up with an old friend

Don't count
the days.
Make the
days count

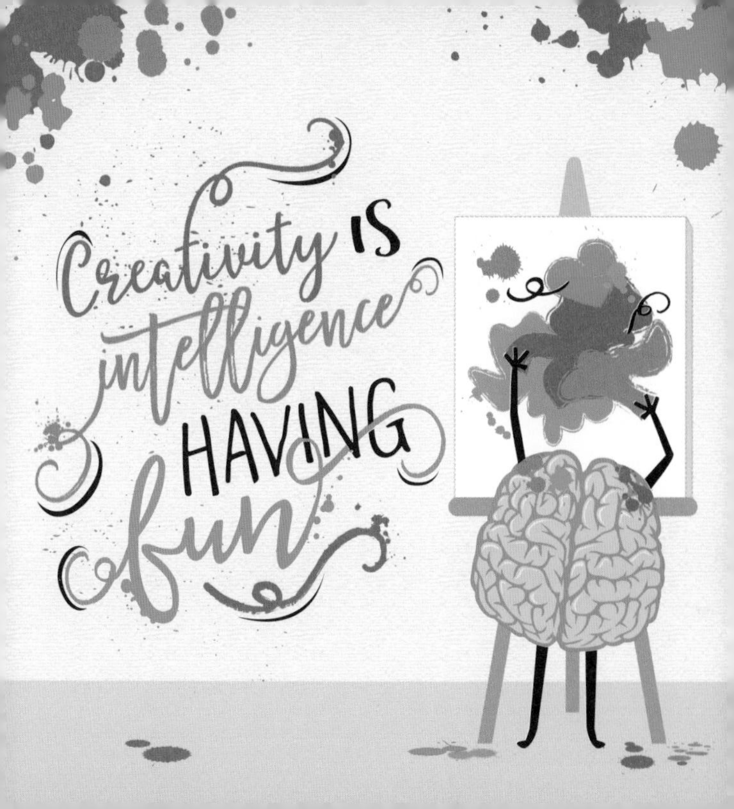
Creativity IS
intelligence
HAVING
fun

EVERY DAY
IS A LITTLE
SWEETER
when CHOCOLATE
IS ON the Menu

LIFE IS TOO
SHORT
TO NOT
EXPRESS
YOURSELF

MAKE SOMEONE ELSE HAPPY,
AND YOUR OWN HAPPINESS
WILL WORK ITSELF OUT

LIFE IS TOO SHORT TO BE bored

you are

SERIOUSLY
GREAT

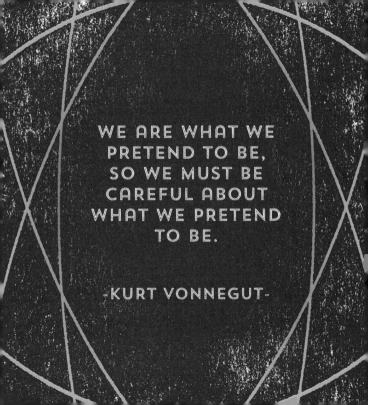

the only

DIFFERENCE *between*

DRAMA

&

COMEDY

is PERSPECTIVE

Be your own YOU!

be a *flamingo* in a flock of pigeons

be a GOOFBALL every once in a while

Do more of what makes you happy

live.
LAUGH.
LOVE.
(REPEAT.)

LIFE ISN'T ABOUT FINDING YOURSELF.
LIFE IS ABOUT CREATING YOURSELF.

—GEORGE BERNARD SHAW—

take time to SMELL the ROSES

you are BRAVER than you BELIEVE, STRONGER than you SEEM, and SMARTER than you THINK.

—A. A. Milne, *Winnie-the-Pooh*

PEOPLE WHO *love* TO EAT ARE THE BEST PEOPLE

-JULIA CHILD

time you enjoy wasting is not wasted time

MARTHE TROLY-CURTIN

EVERYTHING IS BETTER IF IT HAPPENS IN A BLANKET FORT

GRIN

and

SHARE IT

SOMETIMES
ALL IT TAKES
TO TURN A
BAD DAY INTO
A GREAT ONE
IS A LITTLE
POSITIVITY